Five a da

A. L. Griffiths

OLIVER & BOYD

Oliver & Boyd
Longman House
Burnt Mill
Harlow
Essex CM20 2JE

An Imprint of Longman Group UK Ltd

ISBN 0 05 003922 9
First published 1986
Sixth impression 1992

Set in 14pt Linotype Melior Roman
Designed and illustrated by Scorpion Pica
Printed in Hong Kong
CPL/06

The Publisher's policy is to use paper manufactured
from sustainable forests.

MULTIPLICATION

DIVISION

TEMPERATURE

FRACTIONS

LENGTH

TIME

USING A CALCULATOR

CHECKING UP

5 five

1

1 How many mice are there?

2 How many snakes are there?

3 How many ladybirds are there?

4 How many dogs are there?

5 How many tortoises are there?

2

There are 3 in this set.

How many are there in each of these sets?

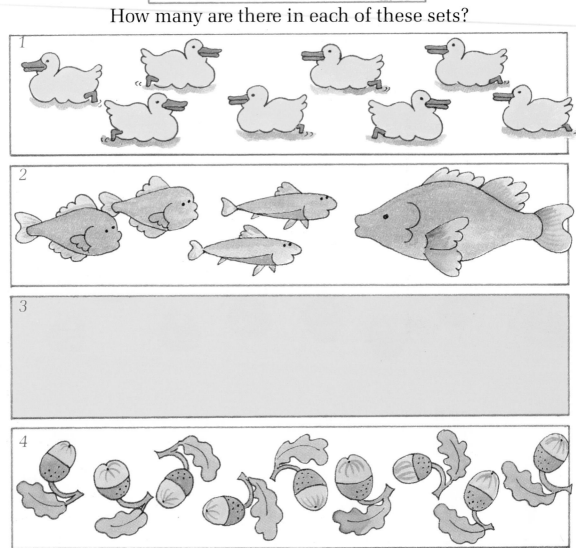

3

1 Which set has 3 members?

2 Which set has the same number as set E?

3 Which sets have 4 members?

4 Which set has more members than set C?

5 Which set has less members than set D?

A

B

C

D

E

F

4

1 The greater set has more members.

Which is the greater set, A or B?

A

B

2 The smaller set has less members.

Which is the smaller set, A or B?

 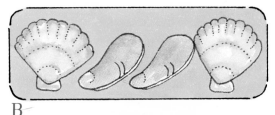

A

B

3 Which is the greater number?

Which is the smaller number?

4 Which of these numbers are greater than 6?

    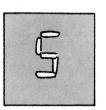

5 Which of these numbers are smaller than 4?

   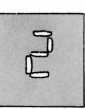

5 *1* Who is second?

2 Who is last?

3 Who is the fifth?

4 What colour is the bird in the middle?

5 What colour is the second last bird?

6 John is first in line.

1 Who is fourth in line?
2 Who is ninth in line?
3 Who is eighth in line?

4 Where is Pete placed?
5 Where is Ann placed?

7 The first day of the week is Sunday.

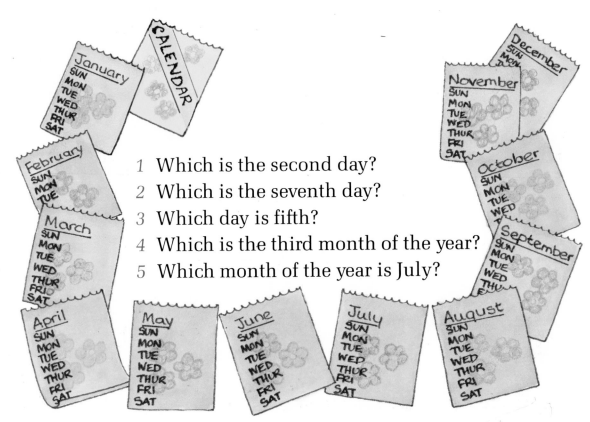

1 Which is the second day?
2 Which is the seventh day?
3 Which day is fifth?
4 Which is the third month of the year?
5 Which month of the year is July?

8 2 more than 7, 2 less than 11, 6 and 3 are all ways of thinking about the number 9. We can say that every number has many names.

Write the 3 names for each number in the circle, like this:

(10)   3 more than 7   3 less than 13   9 and 1

1 (11)   1 more than ☐   2 less than ☐   9 and ☐

2 (9)   2 more than ☐   3 less than ☐   6 and ☐

3 (6)   3 more than ☐   3 less than ☐   1 and ☐

4 (5)   2 more than ☐   1 less than ☐   5 and ☐

5 (8)   4 more than ☐   3 less than ☐   2 and ☐

9

Which of these name the same number as the one in the circle?

1 (7)   2 less than 5   4 more than 3   5 and 0

2 (14)   1 and 4   4 less than 10   10 and 4

3 (10)   1 less than 9   9 and 1   11 more than 1

4 (9)   7 and 3   1 less than 8   2 more than 7

5 (16)   6 less than 10   6 more than 10   6 and 1

10 How many flowers?

1

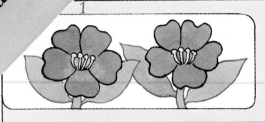 

2 How many children?

3 How many shapes?

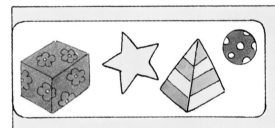 

4 How many animals?

5 How many balloons?

 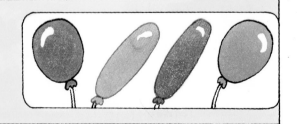

11 Kim has 2 coloured beads and 1 black bead.
How many beads has she altogether?
We could make a drawing, like this:

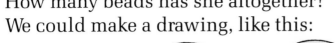

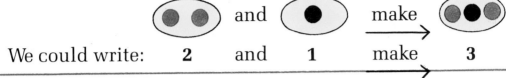

We could write: **2** and **1** make **3**

1 What numeral can we write in place of each △

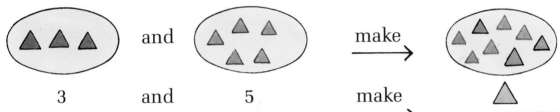

3 and 5 make △

2

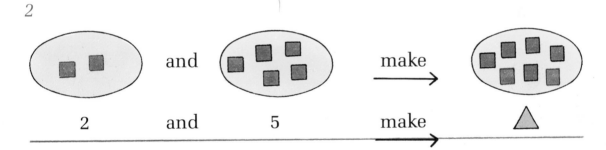

2 and 5 make △

3

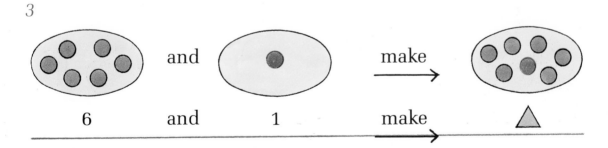

6 and 1 make △

4

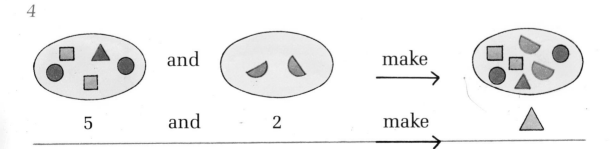

5 and 2 make △

5

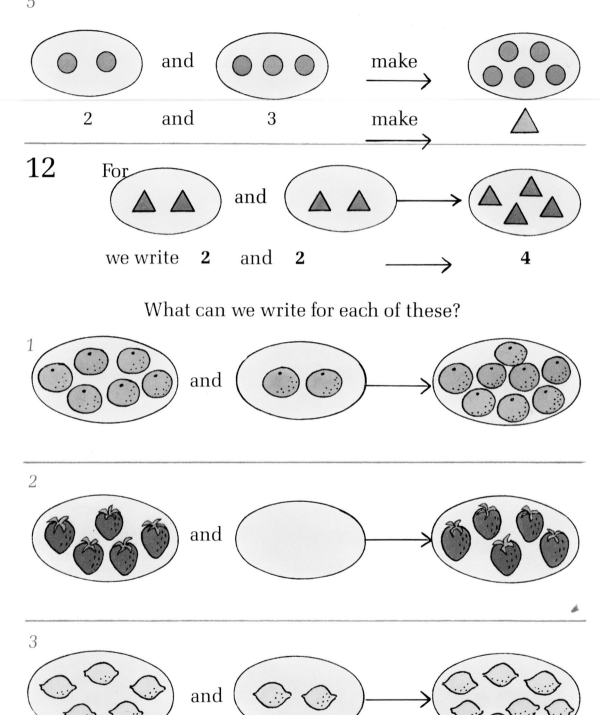

and   and   make

2   and   3   make

12   For

we write   **2**   and   **2**   ⟶   **4**

What can we write for each of these?

1   and

2   and

3   and

4

and

5

and

13 We can add with a number line.
To add 4 and 5
we start at 4 and move 5 places to the right.

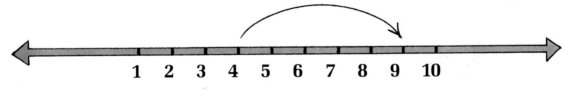

4,5   add   9

Use the number line to find the numeral we should
write in place of each ▲.

We start at	Move to the right	We stop at
4	1 place	5
① 6	2 places	▲
② 4	3 places	▲
③ 2	7 places	▲
④ 3	3 places	▲
⑤ 6	3 places	▲

14

Use this number line to help you.

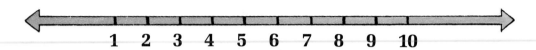

add   add

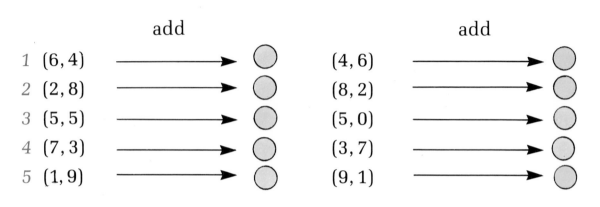

1 (6, 4)   ⟶ ◯   (4, 6)   ⟶ ◯
2 (2, 8)   ⟶ ◯   (8, 2)   ⟶ ◯
3 (5, 5)   ⟶ ◯   (5, 0)   ⟶ ◯
4 (7, 3)   ⟶ ◯   (3, 7)   ⟶ ◯
5 (1, 9)   ⟶ ◯   (9, 1)   ⟶ ◯

15

We can show addition by using the
sign for *addition* +
and the sign for *equals* =.
$2 + 4 = 6$ is an **addition sentence**.

We say: two plus four equals six;
          or: two and four equals six.

Write a numeral in place of each ◯ in these number
sentences. Use the number line to help you, like this:

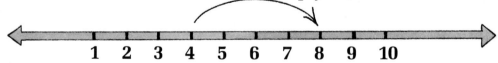

$4 + 4 = 8$ 3 $4 + 5 = ◯$

1 $7 + 1 = ◯$ 4 $3 + 6 = ◯$

2 $5 + 3 = ◯$ 5 $2 + 4 = ◯$

16 It is just as easy to add three numbers, like this:

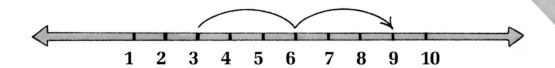

1 2 3 4 5 6 7 8 9 10

3 + 3 + 3 = 9

1 2 + 3 + 2 = ◯

2 5 + 1 + 3 = ◯

3 4 + 1 + 4 = ◯

4 3 + 0 + 1 = ◯

5 4 + 2 + 2 = ◯

17

5 buttons are taken away. How many are left?

3

---

1 6 of these sweets are toffees. How many are not toffees?

---

2 7 of these marbles belong to Mark. How many belong to Ali?

---

3 If 4 of these cars were taken away, how many would be left?

4 If 3 leaves were taken away, how many would be left?

5 If 6 coins were spent, how many would be left?

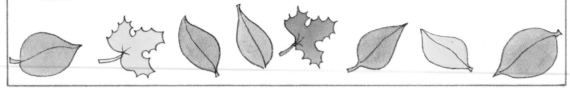

18 Martin has 3 apples and Susan has 2 apples.

Martin has 1 more than Susan.
The *difference* between
3 and 2 is 1.

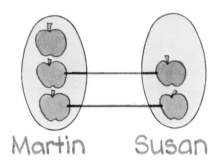

Martin   Susan

1 What is the difference between the number of children and the number of chairs?

2 What is the difference between the number of red beads and the number of black beads?

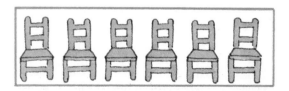

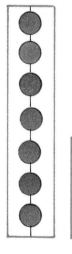

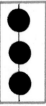

3 What is the difference between the number of
triangles and the number of squares?

 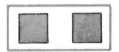

4 What is the difference between the number of
John's coins and the number of Ann's coins?

5 What is the difference between the number of
strawberry cones and the number of plain cones?

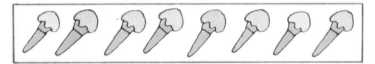 

19

To find the difference between the number of
glasses and the number of cups, we take
the smaller number from the larger number.
We say: **five minus four equals one.** We write: $5 - 4 = 1$
Write a subtraction sentence like this to show the
difference between the number in set A and the number
in set B:

A
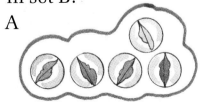  B

$$5 - 5 = 0$$

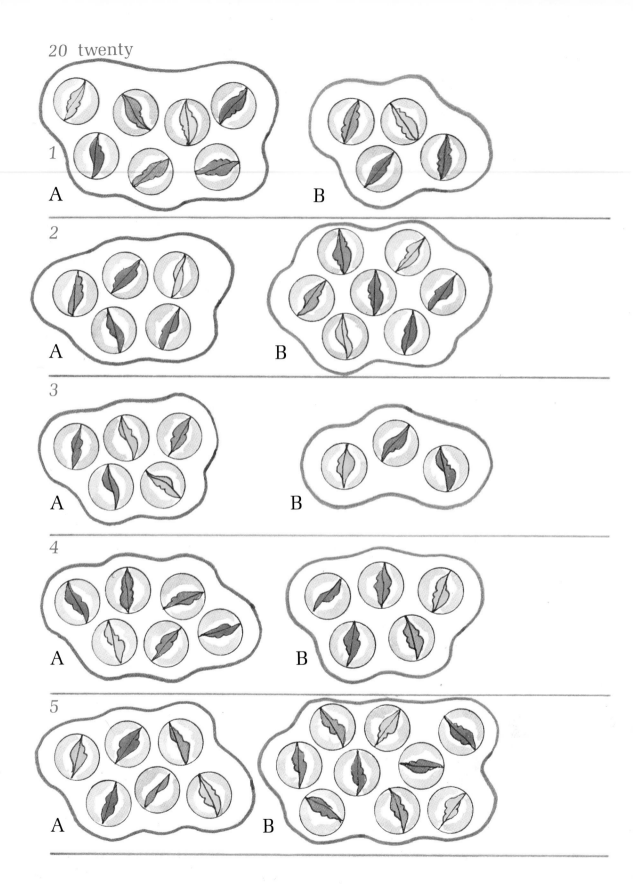

20   Mark had 5 puppies. He sold 3 puppies.
He has 2 puppies left.

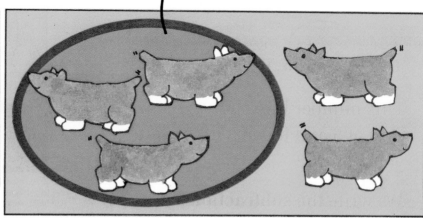

For 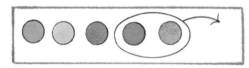 we can write $5 - 2 = 3$

Write out these number sentences in full.

1
 $9 - 6 = $ ▲

2
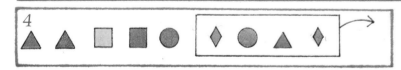 $10 - \blacksquare = $ ▲

3
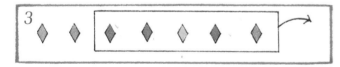 $7 - \blacksquare = $ ▲

4
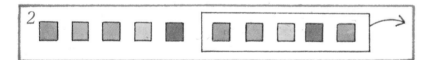 $9 - \blacksquare = $ ▲

5
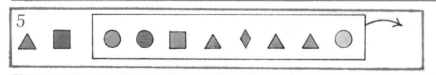 $10 - \blacksquare = $ ▲

21   We can show subtractions
on a number line.

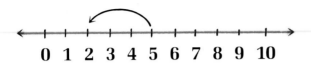

0 1 2 3 4 5 6 7 8 9 10

This number line shows that if you
start at 5 and move 3 to the left,
you stop at 2.

We write the **subtraction sentence:** $5 - 3 = 2$

Write a subtraction sentence for
each of these number lines.

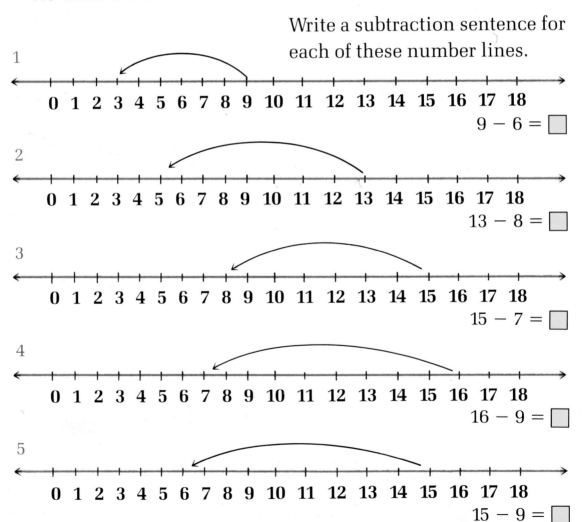

1

0 1 2 3 4 5 6 7 8 9 10 11 12 13 14 15 16 17 18

$9 - 6 = \boxed{}$

2

0 1 2 3 4 5 6 7 8 9 10 11 12 13 14 15 16 17 18

$13 - 8 = \boxed{}$

3

0 1 2 3 4 5 6 7 8 9 10 11 12 13 14 15 16 17 18

$15 - 7 = \boxed{}$

4

0 1 2 3 4 5 6 7 8 9 10 11 12 13 14 15 16 17 18

$16 - 9 = \boxed{}$

5

0 1 2 3 4 5 6 7 8 9 10 11 12 13 14 15 16 17 18

$15 - 9 = \boxed{}$

22 Complete the subtraction sentence
for each drawing.

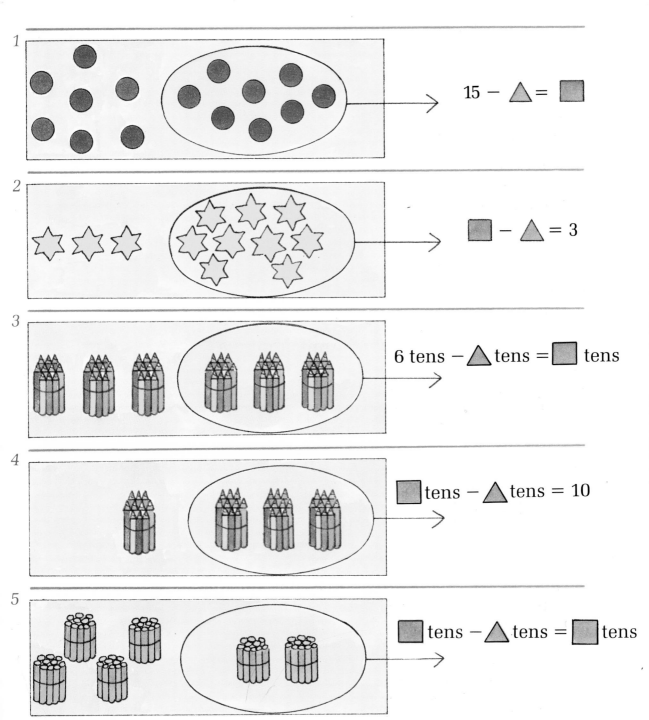

1    $15 - \triangle = \square$

2    $\square - \triangle = 3$

3   6 tens $- \triangle$ tens $= \square$ tens

4    $\square$ tens $- \triangle$ tens $= 10$

5    $\square$ tens $- \triangle$ tens $= \square$ tens

23

$$12 - \boxed{} = 5$$

Think: 12 minus what number is 5?

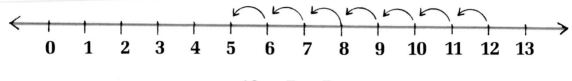

$$12 - 7 = 5$$

---

1 $14 - \boxed{} = 9$ 2 $11 - \boxed{} = 2$ 3 $15 - \boxed{} = 8$

4 $14 - \boxed{} = 7$ 5 $10 - \boxed{} = 4$

---

24   *Think:* what number minus 5 is 7?

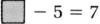

$$\boxed{} - 5 = 7$$

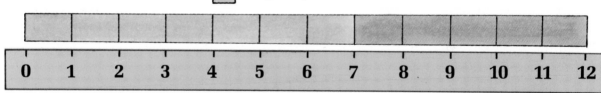

$$12 - 5 = 7$$

---

1 $\boxed{} - 4 = 9$ 2 $\boxed{} - 8 = 4$ 3 $\boxed{} - 9 = 8$

4 $\boxed{} - 7 = 4$ 5 $\boxed{} - 7 = 9$

25

Had 5   Took out 2   Left 3

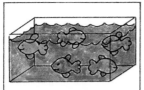 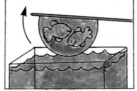 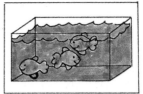

Write the missing numerals.

	Had		Took out		Left
1	14	−	6	=	☐
2	17	−	☐	=	9
3	☐	−	4	=	9
4	16	−	☐	=	7
5	☐	−	9	=	8

---

26   *Think:* 7 plus what number is 13?

$$7 + \boxed{} = 13$$

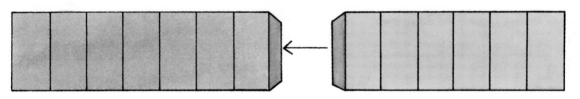

$$7 + 6 = 13$$

---

1 $9 + \boxed{} = 17$ *2* $9 + \boxed{} = 13$ *3* $5 + \boxed{} = 12$

4 $3 + \boxed{} = 11$ *5* $6 + \boxed{} = 15$

27

$$\boxed{} + 6 = 11$$

Think: what number plus 6 is 11?

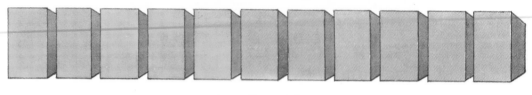

$$5 + 6 = 11$$

1 $\boxed{} + 6 = 13$ 2 $\boxed{} + 8 = 11$ 3 $\boxed{} + 5 = 12$

4 $\boxed{} + 9 = 18$ 5 $\boxed{} + 6 = 14$

28

 7 < 9 is a number sentence.
It says 7 is less than 9.
5 > 3 is a number sentence.
It says 5 is more than 3.

Write >, < or = for each ◯.

1 $7 + 4$ ◯ 10 2 $9 + 3$ ◯ 14 3 $6 + 2$ ◯ $3 + 5$
4 $14 - 7$ ◯ $8 - 1$ 5 $8 + 6$ ◯ $4 + 9$

29   Write >, < or = for each ◯.

1 $7 - 3$ ◯ $10 - 7$ 2 $7 - 4$ ◯ $8 - 5$
3 $9 + 2$ ◯ $6 - 5$ 4 $7 + 0$ ◯ $8 - 1$ 5 $7 + 3$ ◯ $2 + 9$

30

Read the problem, then write a number sentence.

Peter had 5.
He bought 3 more.
How many has he now?

5 + 3 = 8

Sam had 8.
He lost 3.
How many has he now?

8 − 3 = 5

---

1 Sue had 8.
She gave away 4.
How many has she left?

---

2 John had 7.
He was given 3 more.
How many has he now?

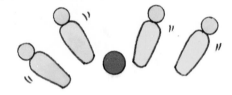

---

3 9 pins were standing.
4 were knocked down.
How many are standing now?

---

4 Lisa bought 12.
She used 6.
How many has she left?

---

5 Sue Lin picked 5.
Karen picked 9.
How many did they pick altogether?

---

31 A graph

The graph shows the number of books each of the children read during a month.

Books read

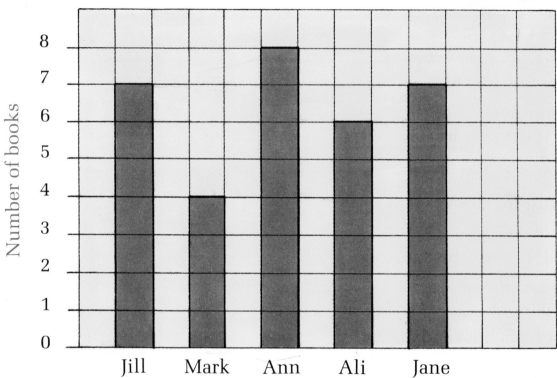

1 Two girls read the same number of books.

Who were they?

2 Who has read 3 more books than Mark?

3 How many books did the boys read in all?

4 How many books did the girls read in all?

5 a Who read 2 more books than Ali?

b Who read 2 fewer books than Ali?

32   Write the missing numerals.

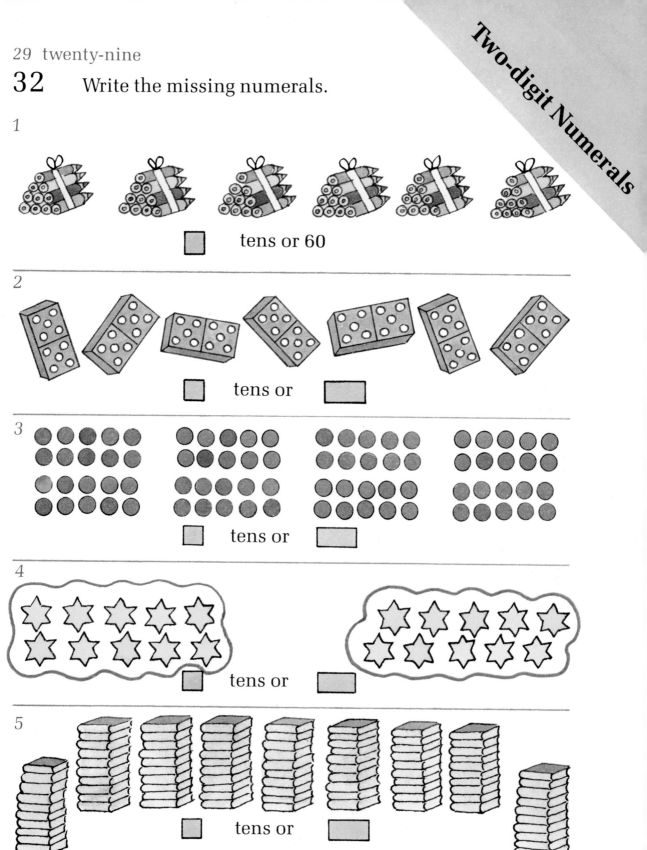

1

□ tens or 60

2

□ tens or ▭

3

□ tens or ▭

4

□ tens or ▭

5

□ tens or ▭

For this number of rods we can write

7 tens and 4 or 74.

Now write out the number sentences below
putting in the numerals.

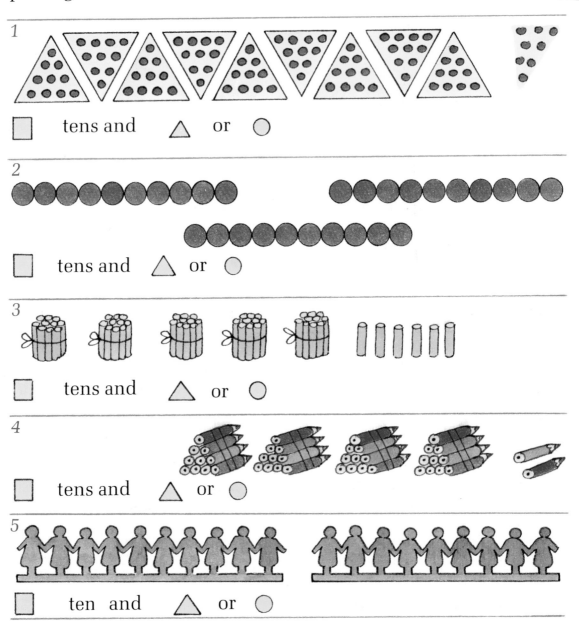

1

☐   tens and   △   or   ○

2

☐   tens and   △   or   ○

3

☐   tens and   △   or   ○

4

☐   tens and   △   or   ○

5

☐   ten and   △   or   ○

34   Write the missing numerals, like this:

1 ten + 1 unit = 11

1 3 tens and 9 units = ☐   *2* 80 + 7 = ☐

3 sixty-eight = ☐   *4* nineteen = ☐

5 9 tens and 6 units = ☐

35

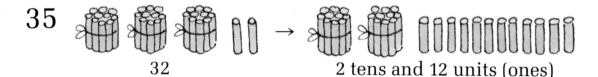

32   2 tens and 12 units (ones)

1   27 → 1 ten and ☐ units

2   56 → 4 tens and ☐ units

3   70 → 6 tens and ☐ units

4   34 → 2 tens and ☐ units

5   93 → 8 tens and ☐ units

36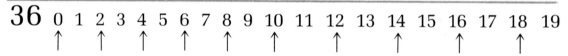

even numbers	odd numbers
The digit in the units place is always 0, 2, 4, 6 or 8.	The digit in the units place is always 1, 3, 5, 7 or 9.

1 Name the even numbers between 7 and 17.

2 Name the odd numbers between 4 and 14.

3 Which of the numbers below are odd numbers?

   30   41   21   13   55   15   78   18   81

4 Choose any even number. Add 1. Is the answer odd or even?

5 Choose any odd number less than 10. Add 1.
    Is the answer odd or even?

37 Numbers can be shown on a counting board
by using counters, or small shells, or pebbles,
or by drawing, like this:

tens	units
● ●	●
● ●	●

We can write a
numeral in digits
42, or words
forty-two.

tens	units
●	● ●
●	● ●

The number shown
on this counting board
is **24** in digits,
twenty-four in words.

Write the
numeral in
digits for each
of these.

1
tens	units
●	● ● ●
● ●	● ● ●

2
tens	units
●	●
●	●
●	●

3
tens	units
● ● ●	
● ● ●	

4
tens	units
	● ● ●
●	● ● ●
	● ● ●

5
tens	units
	● ● ●
	● ● ●
	●

38 Write the
numeral in words
for each of these.

1
tens	units
●	●	●
	●	●
●	●	●

2
tens	units
●	● ● ●
●	● ● ●
●	

3
tens	units
●	●	●	●
	●	●	
●	●	●	●

4
tens	units
● ● ●	
● ● ●	

5
tens	units
● ● ●	● ● ●
● ● ●	● ● ●
● ● ●	● ● ●

39 With two counters, I can show these numbers.

tens	units
●	●

11

tens	units
● ●	

20

tens	units
	● ●

2

1 Write in digits the greatest number I could show with three counters.

2 What is the greatest number I could show with four counters?

3 What is the greatest odd number I could show with four counters?

4 What is the smallest even number I could show with five counters?

5 What is the smallest number I could show with eleven counters?

40 Think of a number which is . . .

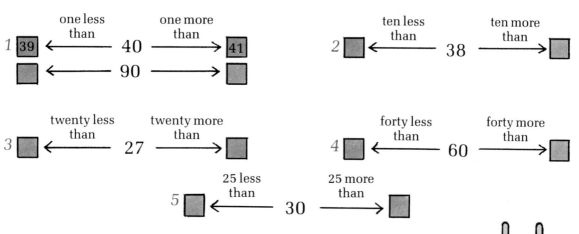

1
$$39 \xleftarrow{\text{one less than}} 40 \xrightarrow{\text{one more than}} 41$$
$$\Box \xleftarrow{\hspace{1cm}} 90 \xrightarrow{\hspace{1cm}} \Box$$

2
$$\Box \xleftarrow{\text{ten less than}} 38 \xrightarrow{\text{ten more than}} \Box$$

3
$$\Box \xleftarrow{\text{twenty less than}} 27 \xrightarrow{\text{twenty more than}} \Box$$

4
$$\Box \xleftarrow{\text{forty less than}} 60 \xrightarrow{\text{forty more than}} \Box$$

5
$$\Box \xleftarrow{\text{25 less than}} 30 \xrightarrow{\text{25 more than}} \Box$$

41 Here is an abacus. It is like a counting board, but this time we use beads and place them on wires. Write the numbers shown below in words.

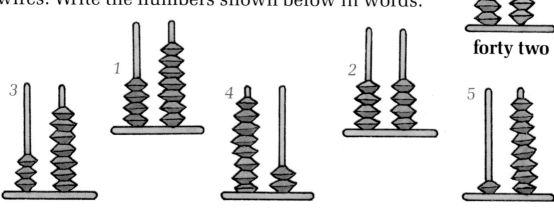

forty two

42

1 Write this numeral in words.

2 Write the two-digit numeral with 7 in the tens place
and 8 in the units place.

3 Write the two-digit numeral with 9 in the units
place and 5 in the tens place.

4 Write the numeral for 10 less than 100.

5   What must I add to this number to make fifty?

---

43   Write the correct sign, $>$ or $<$ or $=$
in place of each ◯.

    1 74 ◯ 4 tens and 7 ones   2 80 ◯ 50 + 20

    3 19 ◯ 20 + 9   4 35 ◯ thirty and 5 ones

    5 40 + 9 ◯ 50 − 1

---

44   10 + 30 = ☐

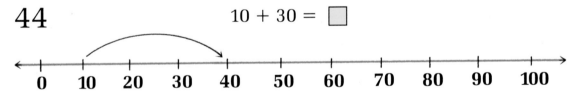

      1 ten + 3 tens is how many tens?

1 30 + 40 = ☐   4 30 + 30 + 20 = ☐

2 40 + 20 = ☐   5 40
                                 +50
                                 ──

3 50 + 10 = ☐   ☐

45

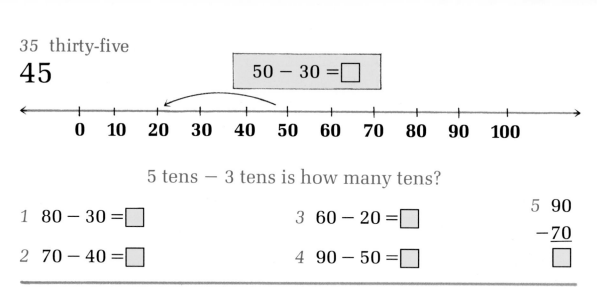

$$50 - 30 = \square$$

5 tens − 3 tens is how many tens?

1 $80 - 30 = \square$

2 $70 - 40 = \square$

3 $60 - 20 = \square$

4 $90 - 50 = \square$

5 $\begin{array}{r} 90 \\ -\underline{70} \\ \square \end{array}$

46 Use the number line to help you find the number which can be put in place of each $\square$ in the number sentences below.

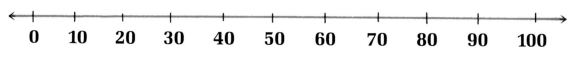

1 $70 - \square = 40$

2 $40 + \square = 90$

Write >, < or = in place of each ⬤.

3 $40 + 40 \ ⬤ \ 90 - 10$

4 $30 + 20 \ ⬤ \ 90 - 50$

5 $60 - 20 \ ⬤ \ 90 - 40$

47

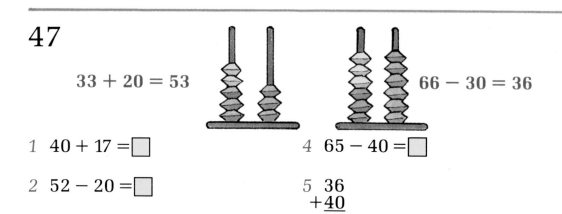

$33 + 20 = 53$

$66 - 30 = 36$

1 $40 + 17 = \square$

2 $52 - 20 = \square$

3 $37 + 50 = \square$

4 $65 - 40 = \square$

5 $\begin{array}{r} 36 \\ +\underline{40} \\ \square \end{array}$

48

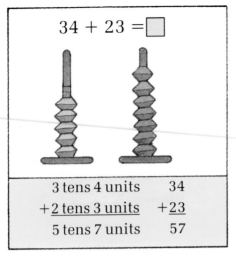

$34 + 23 = \square$

3 tens 4 units	34
+2 tens 3 units	+23
5 tens 7 units	57

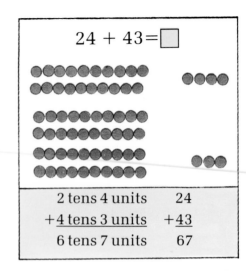

$24 + 43 = \square$

2 tens 4 units	24
+4 tens 3 units	+43
6 tens 7 units	67

1 $64 + 21 = \square$

2 $31 + 12 = \square$

3 $\begin{array}{r} 45 \\ +23 \\ \hline \square \end{array}$

4 $\begin{array}{r} 62 \\ +17 \\ \hline \square \end{array}$

5 $76 + 23 = \square$

---

49 Find the sums:

1 $\begin{array}{r} 34 \\ +45 \\ \hline \square \end{array}$

2 $\begin{array}{r} 52 \\ +47 \\ \hline \square \end{array}$

3 $\begin{array}{r} 56 \\ +31 \\ \hline \square \end{array}$

4 Seventy-six and twelve $= \square$

5 Twenty-one and eleven $= \square$

50

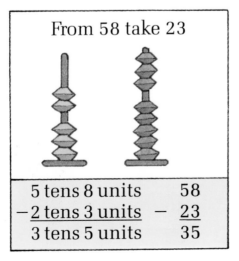

From 58 take 23

5 tens 8 units	58
−2 tens 3 units	− 23
3 tens 5 units	35

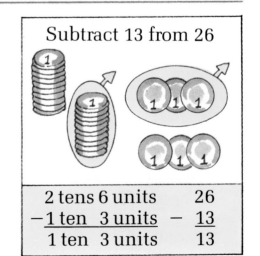

Subtract 13 from 26

2 tens 6 units	26
−1 ten 3 units	− 13
1 ten 3 units	13

1 71 −11 = ☐   *2* 53 −32 = ☐

3 28
−15
☐

4 47
−26
☐

5 84
−62
☐

---

51   Find the difference.
43 and 32

4 tens 3 units

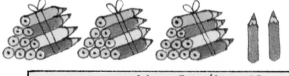

3 tens 2 units

4 tens 3 units	43
3 tens 2 units −	32
difference 1 ten 1 unit	11

Find the differences.

1 38 and 11   *2* 76 and 22

3 67
−34
☐

4 89
−26
☐

5 47
−15
☐

52

1 Martin has 47 picture cards and Sam has 26.
How many more picture cards has Martin than Sam?
2 Tom had twelve marbles. He won 16 more.
How many does he have now?
3 This is the set of coins
in Ann's purse. If she
spent 13 pence, how
many pence has she left?

4 In our school hall there are 53 steel chairs and
   36 wooden chairs. How many chairs are there altogether?

5 David put 17 coins in his album. He has space for 32
   more coins. How many coins will his album hold altogether?

53

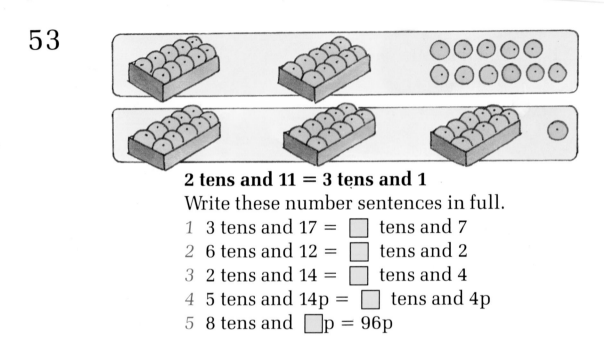

2 tens and 11 = 3 tens and 1
Write these number sentences in full.
1 3 tens and 17 = ☐ tens and 7
2 6 tens and 12 = ☐ tens and 2
3 2 tens and 14 = ☐ tens and 4
4 5 tens and 14p = ☐ tens and 4p
5 8 tens and ☐p = 96p

54 Susan had 26 beads in one box and 7 beads in another box.
How many beads did she have altogether?

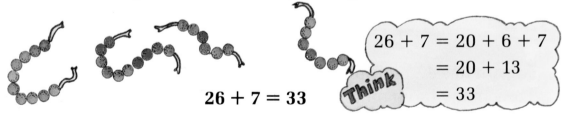

$26 + 7 = 20 + 6 + 7$
$= 20 + 13$
$= 33$

26 + 7 = 33 *Think*

Find the sums:

1 $36 + 7 =$ ☐   2 $9 + 34 =$ ☐

3 $68 + 6 =$ ☐   4 $18 + 8 =$ ☐

5 $64 + 16 =$ ☐

55

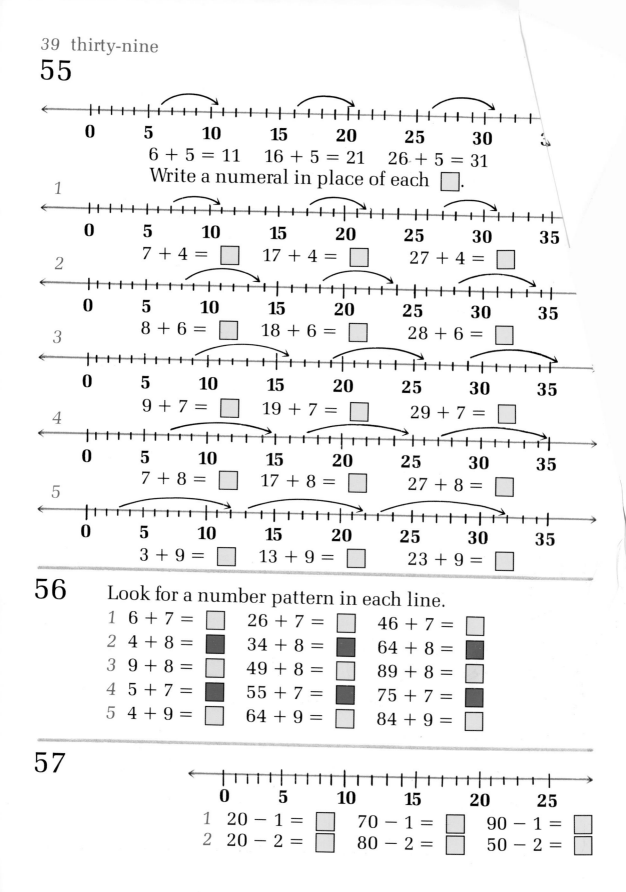

6 + 5 = 11   16 + 5 = 21   26 + 5 = 31

Write a numeral in place of each ▢.

1   7 + 4 = ▢   17 + 4 = ▢   27 + 4 = ▢

2   8 + 6 = ▢   18 + 6 = ▢   28 + 6 = ▢

3   9 + 7 = ▢   19 + 7 = ▢   29 + 7 = ▢

4   7 + 8 = ▢   17 + 8 = ▢   27 + 8 = ▢

5   3 + 9 = ▢   13 + 9 = ▢   23 + 9 = ▢

56

Look for a number pattern in each line.

1   6 + 7 = ▢   26 + 7 = ▢   46 + 7 = ▢
2   4 + 8 = ▢   34 + 8 = ▢   64 + 8 = ▢
3   9 + 8 = ▢   49 + 8 = ▢   89 + 8 = ▢
4   5 + 7 = ▢   55 + 7 = ▢   75 + 7 = ▢
5   4 + 9 = ▢   64 + 9 = ▢   84 + 9 = ▢

57

1   20 − 1 = ▢   70 − 1 = ▢   90 − 1 = ▢
2   20 − 2 = ▢   80 − 2 = ▢   50 − 2 = ▢

Money

3	20 − 3 = ☐	30 − 3 = ☐	60 − 3 = ☐
4	20 − 4 = ☐	70 − 4 = ☐	80 − 4 = ☐
5	20 − 5 = ☐	60 − 5 = ☐	90 − 5 = ☐

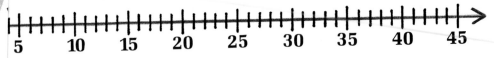

5   10   15   20   25   30   35   40   45

…number line to help you find the missing numerals.

1	17 − 8 = ☐	27 − 8 = ☐	37 − 8 = ☐
2	16 − 9 = ■	26 − 9 = ■	36 − 9 = ■
3	13 − 8 = ☐	33 − 8 = ☐	63 − 8 = ☐
4	13 − 6 = ■	43 − 6 = ■	73 − 6 = ■
5	16 − 7 = ☐	56 − 7 = ☐	96 − 7 = ☐

…9

How many pence?

We think:

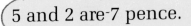

5 and 2 are 7 pence.

We write: 7p.

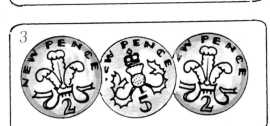

1

2

3

4

5

60

 Ann

1 How much has Ann?

 Mark

2 How much has Mark?

 Ravi

3 How much has Ravi?

 Sue Lin

4 How much has Sue Lin?

 Sarah

5 How much has Sarah?

61   How many pence?

13 pence
We write 13p.

62

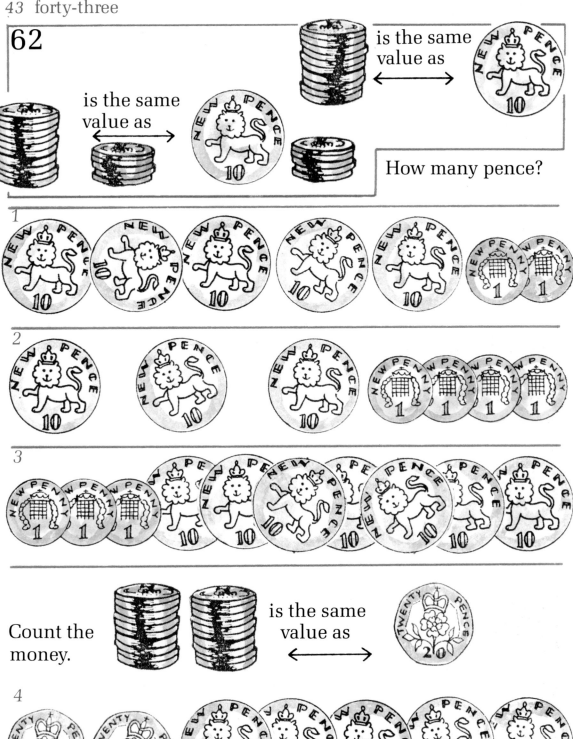

is the same value as

is the same value as

How many pence?

Count the money.

is the same value as

63

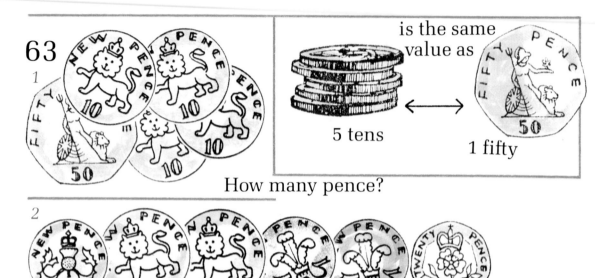

is the same value as

5 tens $\longleftrightarrow$ 1 fifty

How many pence?

64

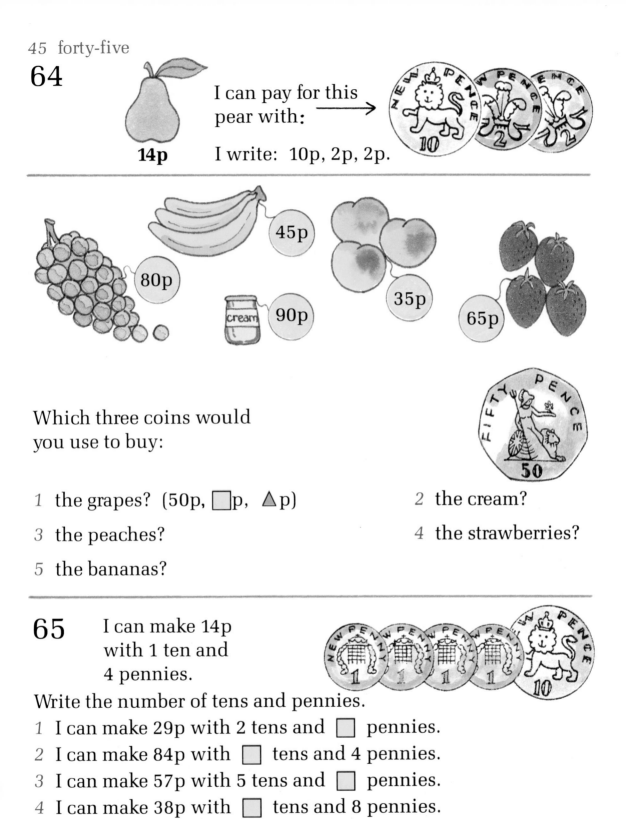

I can pay for this pear with: →

14p

I write: 10p, 2p, 2p.

80p

45p

90p

cream

35p

65p

Which three coins would you use to buy:

1 the grapes? (50p, ☐p, △p)

2 the cream?

3 the peaches?

4 the strawberries?

5 the bananas?

65 I can make 14p with 1 ten and 4 pennies.

Write the number of tens and pennies.

1 I can make 29p with 2 tens and ☐ pennies.

2 I can make 84p with ☐ tens and 4 pennies.

3 I can make 57p with 5 tens and ☐ pennies.

4 I can make 38p with ☐ tens and 8 pennies.

5 I can make 46p with ☐ twenties and 6 pennies.

66

1 What is the cost of the book and the buffers?

2 How much would it cost to buy the buffers and the signal?

3 Find the cost of buying the book and the tunnel.

4 What is the total cost of the bridge and the book?

5 How much must be paid for the bridge and the signal?

67

Find the cost of:

1 the level crossing and tunnel.

2 the level crossing and book.

3 the buffers, lamp and signal.

4 the lamp, book and tunnel.

5 the lamp, book and bridge.

68   Lisa had 7 pennies. She spent 3.
How many had she left?
We could draw this:

Or we could write a number sentence: **7p − 3p = 4p**

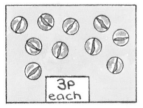 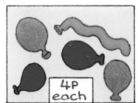 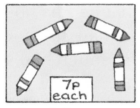 

Write a number sentence for each of these.

1 How much had Karen left out of 9p after buying a balloon?
2 How much had Tom left out of 10p after buying a marble?
3 How much had Kevin left out of 8p after buying a crayon?
4 How much had Sue left out of 10p after buying a pencil?
5 How much had Ravi left out of 10p after buying a marble
   and a balloon?

69

What change did
I get?

 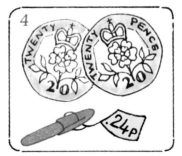 

70

1 Sue Lin had 40p and bought a balloon. How much had she left?

2 Mark needed 7p more to buy a bag of marbles. How much did he have?

3 How much more is the bag of marbles than the balloon?

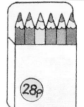

4 Tom got 33p change out of a fifty. What had he bought?

5 Jane had 35p and bought crayons. How much had she left?

71

How many apples are there altogether?

I can write an addition sentence: **4 + 4 = 8**

3 + 3 + 3 + 3 + 3 = 15

Write an addition sentence like the one above for each of these pictures.

1

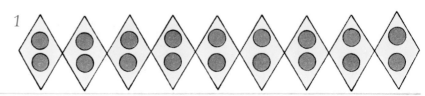

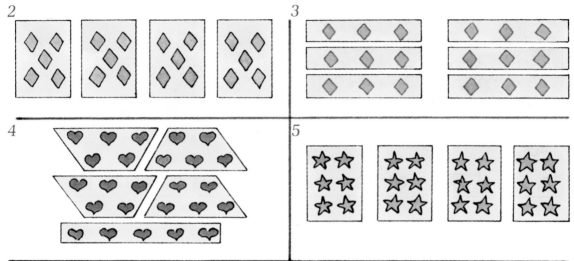

2   3

4   5

72   How many pencils do Ann, Sue and Jane have altogether?

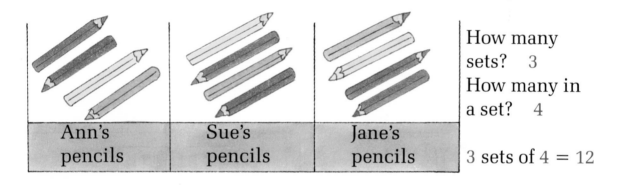

| Ann's pencils | Sue's pencils | Jane's pencils |

How many sets?   3
How many in a set?   4

3 sets of 4 = 12

Use the pictures to help you to write out the number sentences in full.

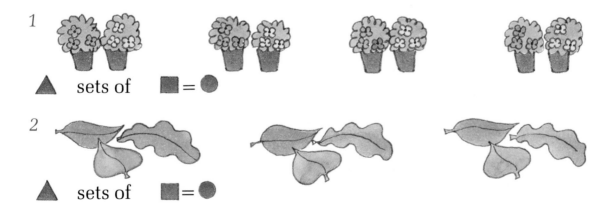

1

▲   sets of   ■ = ●

2

▲   sets of   ■ = ●

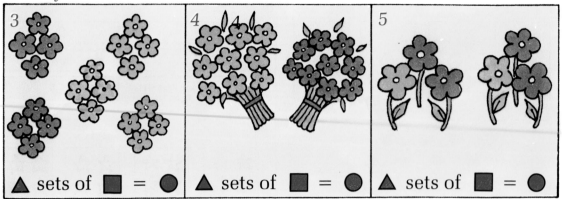

3	4	5
▲ sets of ■ = ●	▲ sets of ■ = ●	▲ sets of ■ = ●

73

We can write
2 sets of 6 = 12

as an addition sentence:
6 + 6 = 12

or a multiplication sentence:
2 x 6 = 12

Write a multiplication sentence for each of these pictures.

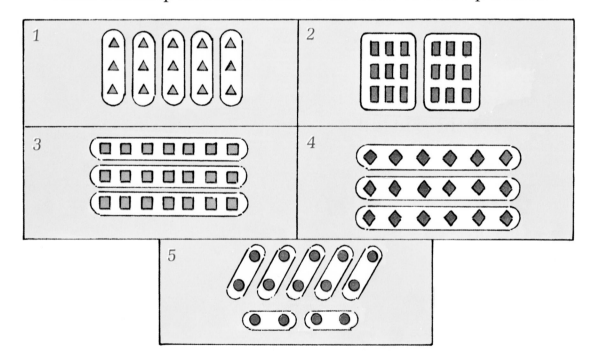

74 Find the answers to these additions.
Then write a multiplication sentence for each,
like this:

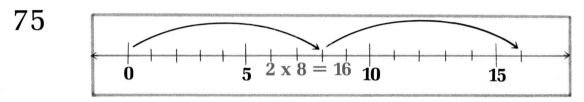

3 + 3 + 3 + 3 + 3 + 3 = 18   or 6 x 3 = 18

1 2 + 2 + 2 + 2 = ■   *2* 5 + 5 + 5 = ■   *3* 7 + 7 + 7 = ■

4 4 + 4 + 4 + 4 = ■   *5* 3 + 3 + 3 + 3 + 3 + 3 + 3 + 3 = ■

75

2 x 8 = 16

Use the number lines to find the numerals which can be
written in place of each ■.

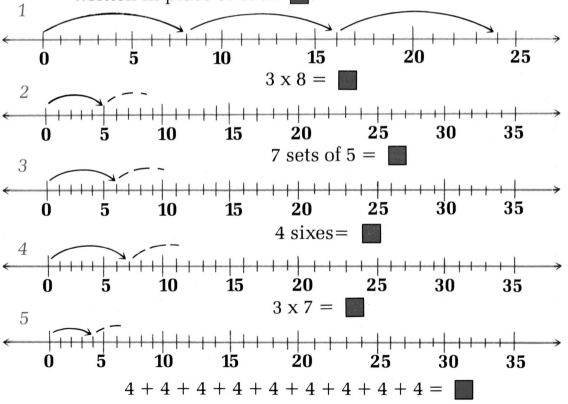

1

3 x 8 = ■

2

7 sets of 5 = ■

3

4 sixes = ■

4

3 x 7 = ■

5

4 + 4 + 4 + 4 + 4 + 4 + 4 + 4 + 4 = ■

76

1 5 threes = ☐ fives   2 1 five = ☐ ones

3 4 threes = ☐ twos   4 2 fours = ☐ twos

5 4 fours = ☐ twos

77

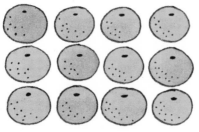 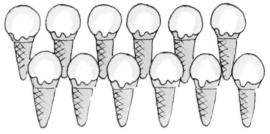

I see 3 sets of 4   I see 2 sets of 6
3 x 4 = **12**   2 x 6 = **12**
           and   and
I see 4 sets of 3   I see 6 sets of 2
4 x 3 = **12**   6 x 2 = **12**

Write a numeral in place of each ☐.

1 3 x 4 = 4 x ☐   2 6 x 2 = ☐ x 6

3 4 x 3 = 6 x ☐   4 2 x ☐ = 4 x 3

5 8 x 7 = 7 x ☐

78

Think > means **is greater than**.
           < means **is less than**.

Write >, < or = in place of each ⬤.
Use the number line to help you.

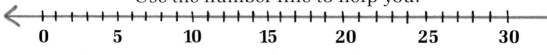

1 4 x 7 ⬤ 7 x 4   2 7 x 3 ⬤ 4 x 5

3 6 x 3 ⬤ 6 + 6 + 6   4 3 x 4 ⬤ 4 + 4 + 4

5 6 x 4 ⬤ 5 x 5

79

1 How many cakes are there altogether in all the boxes?

2 There are 5 cars with 4 people in each car. How many people are there in all?

3 There are 4 boxes of crayons and there are 7 crayons in each box.
How many crayons are there altogether?

4 There are 6 teams with 5 players in each. How many players are there altogether?

5 There are 8 rows of stamps and there are 10 stamps in each row. How many stamps are there in all?

80

Sue Tom Sam Rani Ann

1 Sue, Tom, Sam, Rani and Ann each had the same number of jam tarts. How many jam tarts did they have altogether?

2 In Class 1, 7 pupils each sold 4 tickets for a school concert. How many tickets did they sell?

3 Sue went to France on a 3-week holiday. How many days was she there?

4 Emma and Lisa each bought two balloons. The balloons cost 5p each. How much did they spend in all?

5 There are 3 red pencils, 2 blue pencils and 5 yellow pencils in each bundle. How many pencils are there in 10 bundles?

Division

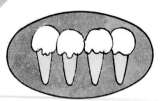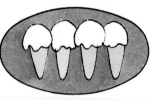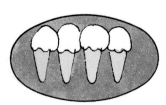

81

There are 12 ice-creams with 4 in each set.

How many fours are there in 12?

We can write: $12 \div 4 = 3$ or $\dfrac{12}{4} = 3$

We say: 12 divided by 4 equals 3

1 a How many threes are there in 6? $6 \div 3 = \square$

  b How many twos are there in 6? $6 \div 2 = \square$

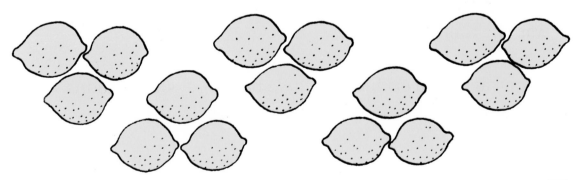

2 a How many fives are there in 15? $15 \div 5 = \square$

  b How many threes are there in 15? $15 \div 3 = \square$

3 a How many sixes are there in 24? $24 \div 6 = \square$

b How many fours are there in 24? $24 \div 4 = \square$

4 a How many threes are there in 18? $\dfrac{18}{3} = \square$

b How many sixes are there in 18? $\dfrac{18}{6} = \square$

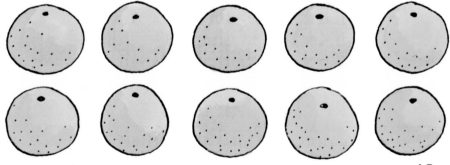

5 a How many twos are there in 10? $\dfrac{10}{2} = \square$

b How many fives are there in 10? $\dfrac{10}{5} = \square$

82   Draw 12 dots. Ring sets of 3.

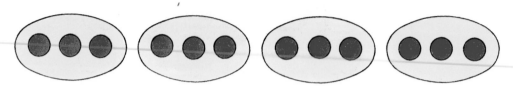

How many threes in 12?

Now write a division sentence, like this: $12 \div 3 = 4$ or $\frac{12}{3} = 4$

1 Draw 18 dots. Ring sets of 6. How many sixes in 18?
Now write a division sentence.

2 Draw 24 dots. Ring sets of 4. How many fours in 24?
Now write a division sentence.

Draw dot pictures to help you with these.
3 $32 \div 4 = \Box$ 4 $36 \div 6 = \Box$ 5 $\frac{40}{5} = \Box$

---

83   We can use multiplication to help us to divide.

Think If $4 \times 3 = 12$, then $12 \div 3 = 4$.

Write out these sentences in full.
1 If $6 \times 3 = 18$, then $18 \div 3 = \Box$
2 If $4 \times 7 = 28$, then $28 \div \Box = 4$
3 If $6 \times 5 = 30$, then $\Box \div 5 = 6$
4 If $4 \times 9 = 36$, then $\Box \div 9 = \triangle$
5 If $5 \times 7 = 35$, then $\Box \div 7 = \triangle$

---

84   How many dots are there altogether?
How many twos?
How many sixes?
Now I can write these sentences:

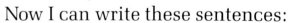

$12 \div 2 = 6$ $\frac{12}{2} = 6$ $12 \div 6 = 2$ $\frac{12}{6} = 2$

Look at these dot pictures and then write out the
number sentences in full.

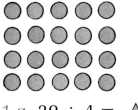

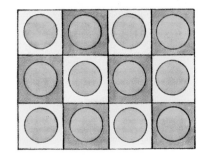

1 a 20 ÷ 4 = △   2 a ☐ ÷ 4 = △   3 a ☐ ÷ 3 = △
  b ☐ ÷ 5 = ◆   b ☐ ÷ 8 = ◆   b ☐ ÷ 6 = ◆

4 a ☐ ÷ 2 = ◆

  b ☐ ÷ 7 = △

5 a $\dfrac{\boxed{}}{3}$ = ◆

  b $\dfrac{\boxed{}}{4}$ = △

---

85   There were enough Christmas tree decorations
      to put 8 on each tree. There were 24 decorations.
      How many trees were there?

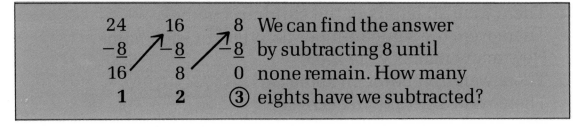

24	16	8	We can find the answer
−8	−8	−8	by subtracting 8 until
16	8	0	none remain. How many
1	**2**	**③**	eights have we subtracted?

Work out these in the same way.
1 Each box holds 6 pencils. How many boxes
   are needed for 24 pencils?
2 There are 5 chocolates in a row. How many rows
   are there in a box of 30 chocolates?
3 How many threes are there in 21?
4 $\dfrac{15}{3}$ = ☐   5 28 ÷ 7 = ☐

86 Use the number lines to find the numerals which can be written in place of each ☐

1

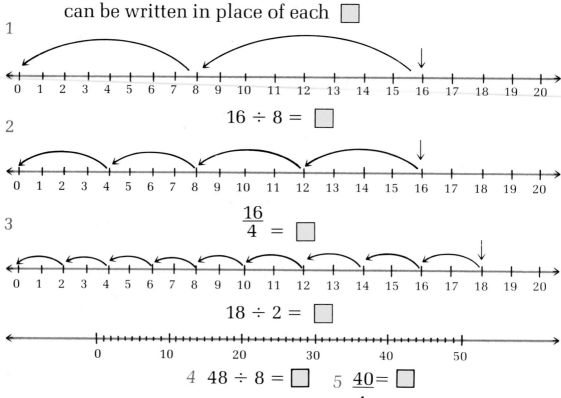

$$16 \div 8 = \square$$

2

$$\frac{16}{4} = \square$$

3

$$18 \div 2 = \square$$

4 $48 \div 8 = \square$ 5 $\frac{40}{4} = \square$

87

1 There were 18 chocolates in a box.
   There were the same number in each row.
   How many rows were there?

2 There were 40 letters in the children's names.
   There were the same number of letters in each name.
   How many names were there?

3 There were 25 people in some cars.
   There were 5 people in each car.
   How many cars were there?

4 Karen spent 36p on pencils.
   The pencils cost 9p each.
   How many pencils did she buy?

5 There were 18 chairs.
   They were placed in 2 equal rows.
   How many chairs were in each row?

88

1 There are 30 books with the same number in each pile. How many piles of books are there?

2 Jane had 42 photographs for her album. She placed 6 photographs on each page. How many pages did she fill?

3 Fifty-five children went on a visit to the Safari Park. They travelled in 5 mini-buses with the same number of children in each. How many pupils were in each mini-bus?

4 Jenny planted 36 beans. She planted them in 6 equal rows. How many beans were in each row?

5 Starting with 21, how many times can we subtract 3?

89

1 A florist had 20 flowers. She placed the same number in each vase. How many did she put in each?

2 Five children played a game of cards. They each had 4 cards and there were 4 left over. How many cards were there altogether?

3 How many crayons are there in 5 boxes?

4 Mrs Grant bought a large block of chocolate with 24 squares. She and her children shared it equally. How many squares did each get?

5 There are 9 rows of these chairs in the school hall. How many chairs are there altogether?

90

0°C   30°C

We measure temperature with a thermometer.
We measure temperature in degrees Celsius.

The temperature shown on the thermometer above
is sixty-two degrees Celsius.
We write 62°C.

What temperature is shown on each of the thermometers
below?

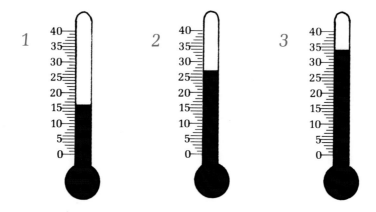

4   The temperature was 17°C. It rose 10°.
    What was it then?

5   The temperature was 40°C. It fell 11°.
    What was it then?

91 This rectangle has two parts the same shape and size.

1 of the 2 parts has been coloured. The coloured part is **half** of the rectangle.

We can write half like this: $\frac{1}{2}$

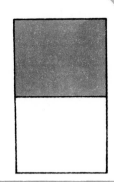

Which pictures show a half?

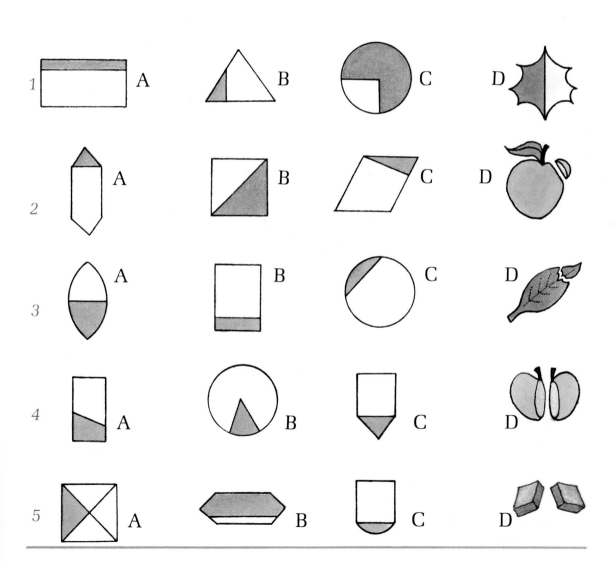

92

1 Which picture shows four equal parts?

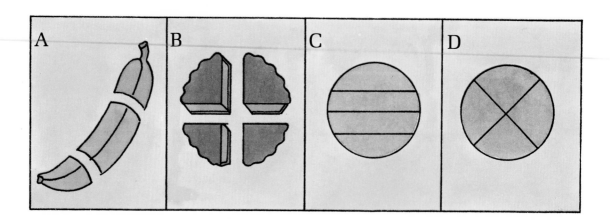

When there are four equal parts, one part
is one fourth or one quarter.
We write: $\frac{1}{4}$

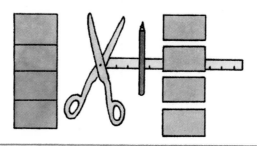

2 Which shape is $\frac{1}{4}$ coloured?

A  B 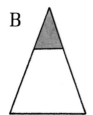 C 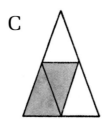 D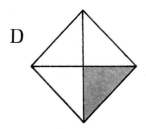

3 Which two shapes are a quarter coloured?

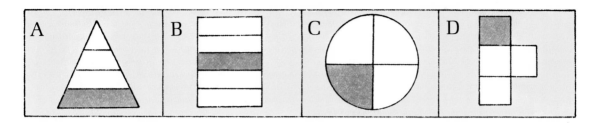

4 Which two shapes are two-fourths coloured?

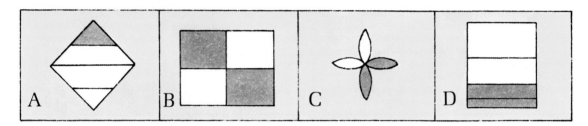

5 Which two shapes are three-quarters coloured?

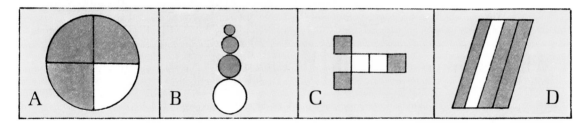

93   How many parts are there?
Are the parts equal in size?

Each part is one-third of the whole.
We write: $\frac{1}{3}$

Two parts are two-thirds.
We write: $\frac{2}{3}$

Which shapes are $\frac{1}{3}$ coloured?

1

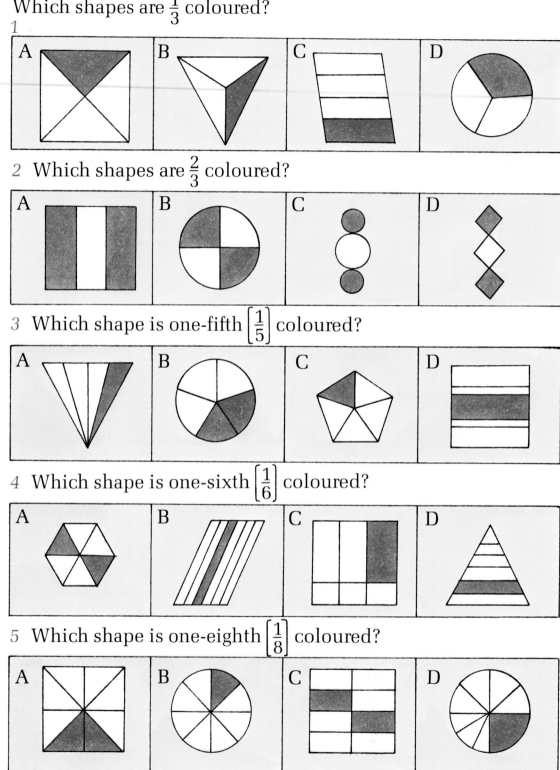

2 Which shapes are $\frac{2}{3}$ coloured?

3 Which shape is one-fifth $\left[\frac{1}{5}\right]$ coloured?

4 Which shape is one-sixth $\left[\frac{1}{6}\right]$ coloured?

5 Which shape is one-eighth $\left[\frac{1}{8}\right]$ coloured?

94

$\frac{1}{3}$ of 6 = 2

6 ÷ 3 = 2

1 Two girls share these cards equally.
Each girl will get $\frac{1}{2}$ of the cards.

$\frac{1}{2}$ of 6 = ☐

2 Four boys share these cherries equally.
Each boy gets $\frac{1}{4}$ of the cherries.

$\frac{1}{4}$ of 16 = ☐

---

3 Three children share these strawberries equally.
Each child will get $\frac{1}{3}$ of the strawberries.

$\frac{1}{3}$ of △ = ☐

4 One-third of these beads belong to Kim.
How many of these beads are Kim's?

5 How many are there in one-fifth of these pencils?

95 Five children shared a box
of chocolates equally.
They each had one-fifth.

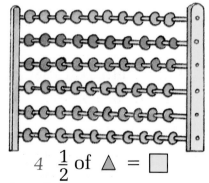

$$\frac{1}{5} \text{ of } 30 = 6$$

Write these number sentences, putting the
correct numerals in place of each △ and ☐.

1 $\frac{1}{4}$ of △ = ☐

2 $\frac{1}{5}$ of △ = ☐

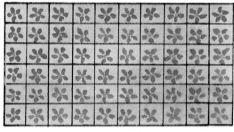

3 $\frac{1}{3}$ of △ = ☐

4 $\frac{1}{2}$ of △ = ☐

5 How many are there in three-quarters of eighty?

96

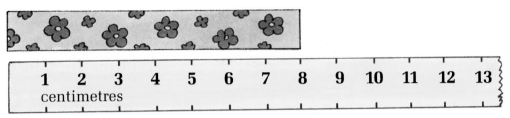

This ribbon is about 8 centimetres long.

We write **8 cm.**

Use your ruler to measure the length of each pencil.

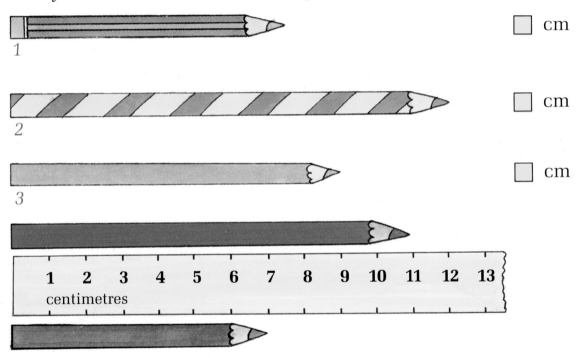

1 ☐ cm

2 ☐ cm

3 ☐ cm

4 How many centimetres longer is the red pencil than the blue pencil?

5 If these two pencils were put together, what would be the total length?   ☐ cm + ◆ cm = △ cm

97 Find the length of the path.

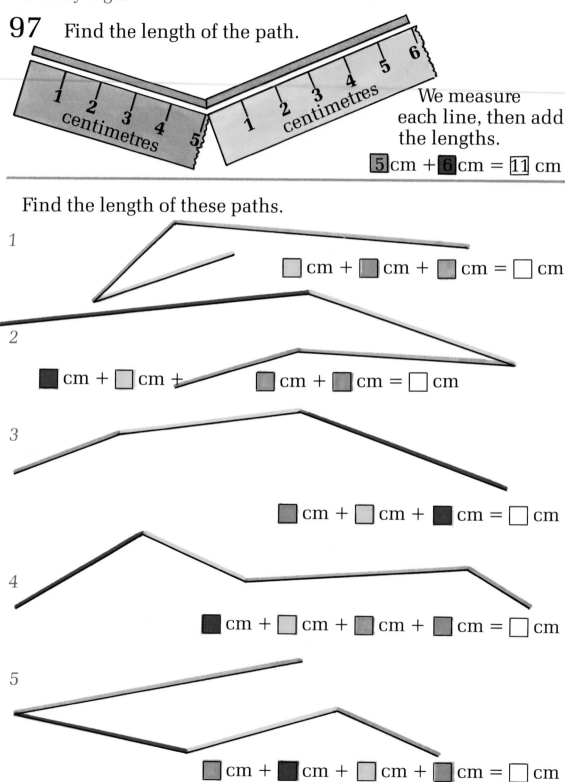

We measure each line, then add the lengths.

5 cm + 6 cm = 11 cm

Find the length of these paths.

1

☐ cm + ☐ cm + ☐ cm = ☐ cm

2

☐ cm + ☐ cm + ☐ cm + ☐ cm = ☐ cm

3

☐ cm + ☐ cm + ☐ cm = ☐ cm

4

☐ cm + ☐ cm + ☐ cm + ☐ cm = ☐ cm

5

☐ cm + ☐ cm + ☐ cm + ☐ cm = ☐ cm

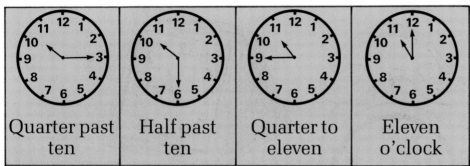

| Quarter past ten | Half past ten | Quarter to eleven | Eleven o'clock |

1 What time does Tim get up?

2 What time does he have breakfast?

3 What time does he leave home?

4 What time does he get to school?

5 What time does he return home?

99 What times are shown on these clocks?

5 Here are some modern clocks without numerals.

What times do they show?

a

b

c

d

100

1

5

Calculating steps

Multiply the number by 3.
Add 6 to the answer.
Divide the sum by 7.
Subtract 2.

2

3

Add 7.

Divide by 2.

Multiply by 3.

Subtract 5.

3

4

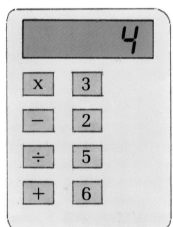

4

26

Add 4.

Divide by 5.

Subtract 3.

Multiply by 10.

5

50

Divide by 10.

Add 4.

Multiply by 2.

Subtract 9.

101

> I am thinking of a number.
> When I add 7 to it, I get 20.
> What is the number?
> $\square + 7 = 20$
>
> The number is 13. $13 + 7 = 20$

1 I am thinking of a number. When I subtract 30 from it, I get 30. What is the number?
2 I am thinking of a number. When I multiply it by 4, I get 24. What is the number?
3 I am thinking of a number. When I divide it by 3, I get 10. What is the number?
4 I am thinking of a number. When I add 9 to it; I get 30. What is the number?
5 I am thinking of a number. When I find $\frac{1}{4}$ of it, the answer is 7. What is the number?

102

1 Add 5 and 5; multiply by 5; subtract 5; divide by 5.

2 Multiply 4 by 3; add 8; divide by 2; subtract 10.

3 Divide 15 by 5; subtract 2; add 7; multiply by 1.

4 Subtract 2 from 20; divide by 2; add 4; multiply by 3.

5 Multiply 9 by 0; add 20; divide by 1; add 0.

103

1 There are 28 dominoes.
How many will each boy get?

2 Tim's brother scored a bull's-eye, an inner ring
and an outer ring. What was his total score?

3 Here are the names of the pupils in Tom's reading
group.　a　What fraction are girls?
　　　　　b　What fraction are boys?

4 A shop started the day with 50 lollipops. Mark and
Lisa bought some. How many were left?

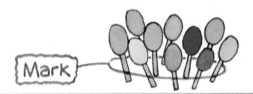 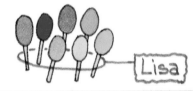

5 This is how Simon kept the score of a road
safety quiz. How many correct answers were there?

104

1 A number has many names. Which of these are names for the number 9?

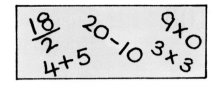

2 Write out this number sentence, putting a numeral in place of ▢.

$$57 = ▢ \text{ tens} + 17 \text{ ones}$$

3 Write >, < or = in place of ◯.

$$12 ÷ 4 ◯ 3 \times 4.$$

4 Write a division sentence for this number line.

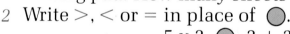

5 Which of these pictures is two-thirds coloured?

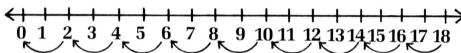

A   B   C   D

105

1 Rani used 19 sheets from her 50-sheet writing pad. How many sheets were left?

2 Write >, < or = in place of ◯.

$$5 \times 3 \ ◯ \ 3 + 3 + 3 + 3 + 3$$

3 What number is 20 more than 65?

4 Write out this number sentence, putting in the correct signs +, −, x or ÷.

$$15 ◯ 3 = 2 ◯ 3$$

5 What is the hidden number?

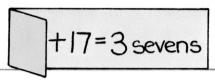

+17 = 3 sevens

106

1 There were 48 pupils in 2 classes.
Each class had the same number.
How many pupils were in each class?

2 There were 77 pupils
and 8 teachers. How
many were there in all?

3 Emma had 90p.
She gave Sarah 16p. How
much did Emma have left?

4 There are 80 books in
a library and there are
20 books on each shelf.
How many shelves are there?

5 There are 14 large chairs
and 66 small chairs.
How many chairs are there
altogether?

107

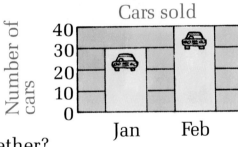

1 a How many cars were sold in
January?
b How many cars were sold in
February?
c How many cars were sold altogether?

2 There were 6 pencils
in a box. There were
10 boxes. How many
pencils were there?

3 There were $\frac{1}{2}$ dozen eggs in a box.
Sue Lin bought 48 eggs.
How many boxes did she buy?

4 There are 15 red crayons,
60 blue crayons
and 15 yellow crayons.
How many crayons
are there in all?

5 The temperature at noon was 30°C.
It dropped 12°, then rose 7°.
What was the temperature?

108

Who am I?

1 If you divide 24 by me,
you get 3.

2 If you add 20 to me,
you get 50.

3 If you subtract 11 from me,
you get 39.

4 If you multiply me
by 8, you get 80.

5 If you add 10 to me, and then
add 5, you get 90.

109

Who am I?

1
Add 30 to me.
You should get 45.

2
First add 11 to me, then
take away 5.
You should have 10.

3
Add me to myself,
then add 1.
You should get 19.

4
Add 6 to me, then
take away 4.
You should have 5.

5
Subtract 9 from me
then subtract 11.
You should have 50.

110

1 Sue counted 20 aircraft on the ground and 9
   aircraft in the air. How many did she count altogether?

2 At Heathrow Airport 60 aircraft took off and 35 aircraft
   landed in an hour. How many more took off than landed?

3 Ali saw 40 British aircraft, 30 United States
   aircraft and 25 other aircraft. How many was this in all?

4 A small jet-liner had 91 passengers. 12 of these
   were children. How many adult passengers were there?

5 A helicopter had seats for 40 passengers. 19 seats
   were empty. How many passengers were on the helicopter?

111   Write these in full.

1 $\frac{1}{4}$ of ☐ = 7   2 4 x 20 = ☐ x 10

3 (7 x 5) + 2 = ☐   4 29 ÷ ☐ = 5 remainder 4

5 (8 x 4) + ☐ = 35

112

1 Lisa gave a fifty and a ten to buy the necklace.
How much change did she get?

2 Sue Lin had 3 tens. She was given 3 twenties.
How much did she have then?

3 Sam had 25p. Mark gave him 3 fives.
How much did Sam have then?

4 Karen had a fifty. She spent 29p. How much did she have left?

5 Ravi had 43p. He was given 17p by his mum.
How much did he have then?

113

1 I have 4 coins that equal 35p. What are the coins?

2 I have 3 coins that equal 71p. One coin is a twenty.

   What are the others?

3 Use 4 coins to make 20p. What are the coins?

4 How many fives are equal in value to 2 twenties?

5 Use the least number of coins to make 72p. Name the coins.